MOTHS

by Sophie Lockwood

Content Adviser: Michael Breed, Ph.D., Professor,
Ecology and Evolutionary Biology,
The University of Colorado, Boulder

THE CHILD'S WORLD®, MANKATO, MINNESOTA

Moths

Published in the United States of America by The Child's World®
1980 Lookout Drive • Mankato, MN 56003-1705
800-599-READ • www.childsworld.com

Acknowledgements:

The Child's World®: Mary Berendes, Publishing Director

The Creative Spark: Mary Francis, Project Director; Wendy Mead, Editor; Deborah Goodsite, Photo Researcher

The Design Lab: Kathleen Petelinsek, Designer, Production Artist, and Cartographer

Photos:

Cover: Daniel Dempster Photography/Alamy; frontispiece: Gary W. Carter /CORBIS; half title and CIP: Janeen Wassink/iStockphoto.com.

Interior: Alamy: 31, (Suzy Bennett); Animals Animals/Earth Scenes: 36, (NANCY ROTENBERG);BigStockPhoto.com: 5, 28 (Willie F. M.); Corbis: 27 (Gary W. Carter); iStockphoto.com: 5, 9 (BMPix), 5, 30 (Joe McDaniel), 11 (Joy Miller), 33 (Eric Gagnon); Minden Pictures: 16, (Michael and Patricia Fogden); Oxford Scientific: 16, (Keith Porter), 18–19 (Densey Clyne), 22 (Waina Cheng); Visuals Unlimited: 12–13, (RMF), 21(Alex Kerstitch), 25, (Leroy Simon), 35 (Gary Meszaros).

Map: The Design Lab: 7.

Library of Congress Cataloging-in-Publication Data

Lockwood, Sophie.
  Moths / by Sophie Lockwood.
    p. cm.—(The world of insects)
  Includes index.
  ISBN-13: 978-1-59296-824-4 (library bound: alk. paper)
  ISBN-10: 1-59296-824-4 (library bound: alk. paper)
  1. Moths—Juvenile literature. I. Title.
  QL544.2.L66 2007
  595.78—dc22   9149   2006103455

TABLE OF CONTENTS

Chapter One

The Miracle of Silk

Five thousand years ago, a Chinese empress made an incredible discovery. Her name was Xiling Shi, and she was the wife of the emperor Huanghi. As she enjoyed a cup of tea in the garden, the empress was stunned when a cocoon dropped into her cup. Slowly, the cocoon unraveled into a long, thin strand of thread—silk.

The Chinese began collecting the cocoons and weaving the threads into silk in about 3,000 BC. It took nearly 1,600 years before silk became a true industry. This unique fabric was sold only by China.

By 100 BC, China had developed a trade route that stretched from Japan to Italy along what came to be known as the Silk Road. Although spices, jade, and other goods traveled from China to Europe, the product of greatest value was silk. That material was so important to China, that its production became a closely guarded secret. Anyone caught smuggling silkworms out of China was put to death.

Did You Know?
It takes 2,100 silkworm cocoons to make a Japanese kimono.

EUROPE

Rome

Mediterranean Sea

AFRICA

Turpan

Anxi

Samarkand

ASIA

Xi'an

Baghdad

30°N

Arabian Sea

Bay of Bengal

South China Sea

15°N

E Q U A T O R

0°

I n d i a n

15°S

O c e a n

N

Land Routes

Sea Routes

30°S

15°E   30°E   45°E   60°E   75°E   90°E   105°E   120°E

The Chinese used the Silk Road to sell their most popular fabric in Europe.

Despite the stiff penalty, China could not keep its secret forever. The king of Khotan, a former kingdom in what is now western China, married a Chinese princess. She decided to bring silk to her new home. The young bride hid silkworm cocoons and mulberry tree seeds in her hair. Silk went to Khotan.

The princess's trickery was the first, but not the only deceit involved in spreading the silk industry westward. In AD 552, Christian travelers to Khotan smuggled silkworm cocoons out of the country in hollow walking sticks. Those cocoons began a silk industry in what is today Turkey.

The silkworm, *Bombyx mori,* if left to its natural path, would become a moth. The remarkably strong, soft, lush fabric that is silk is the wrapping of the silk moth caterpillar's cocoon. These caterpillars eat themselves silly, munching pounds of mulberry leaves during the larval stage.

The majority of silkworms are not allowed to become moths. Their cocoons are thrown into boiling water, which kills the **pupae** and loosens the silk thread. One cocoon yields a single strand of raw silk, measuring up to 900 meters (2,953 feet). Among the traits that make silk so valuable are its strength and its ability to accept dye.

Would You Believe?
About 70 million pounds of raw silk are produced yearly. At about 2,500 cocoons to the pound, that equals 17.5 billion cocoons.

Of course, not all the cocoons can be harvested, or there would be no more silk. The pupae that survive become flightless moths. During their short 10-day life span, the males and females mate. Females lay about 500 eggs, which become exceptionally hungry caterpillars that feed day and night. The caterpillar eats 10,000 times its own weight in less than a month. Chemical changes in the caterpillar signal the time to spin a cocoon. The caterpillar spews clear, sticky fluid from its mouths that dries into silk as soon as it touches the air. Who could have imagined that such richness and beauty could come from a fat white caterpillar and a plain, off-white moth?

A silkworm climbs on a mulberry tree branch.

Chapter Two

The Moth Cycle of Life

Is it a butterfly or a moth? Too many people think that color is the key factor in identifying moths from butterflies. However, dull brown-gray butterflies—like the palm skimmer or the southern cloudy wing—are found in nature. And, there are some stunningly colorful moths, such as the Madagascan sunset moth or Sloane's urania moth. No, it is not color or size that makes a moth a moth.

Moths are highly diverse insects. A few fly by day while most are night creatures. Some are as small as a thumbnail, while others have wingspans as wide 30 centimeters (1 foot). What most moths have in common are **antennae** with fuzzy ends, and larger, thicker bodies than butterflies. Usually—but not always—the forewings are broader than the hind wings. At rest, moth wings fold down like a fan covering the moth's back, while butterfly wings line up along their backs.

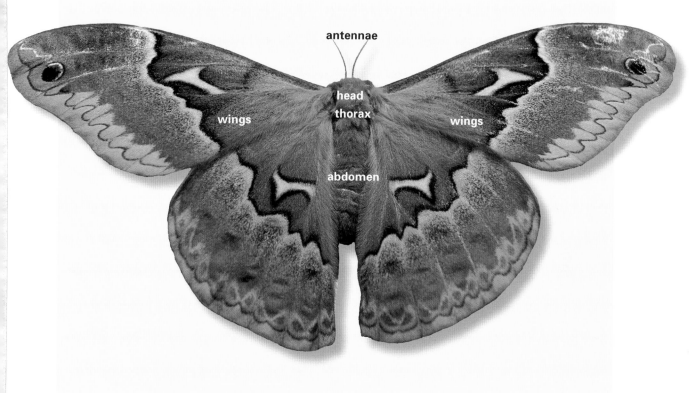

antennae

head
thorax

wings

wings

abdomen

BODY PARTS

Moths have all the classic elements of insects: a three-part body and six legs. The body has a head, a **thorax**, and an **abdomen**. The most noticeable part of moths has to be the wings.

A moth's head features a set of compound eyes, antennae, and usually a **proboscis**. The eyes have 12,000 to 17,000 separate **facets**—called **ommatidia**. Each facet is like an extremely tiny individual eye. The eyes allow moths to see size, shape, movement, and a range of color including ultraviolet light. The human eye can see a

A moth's wings are several times larger than its body.

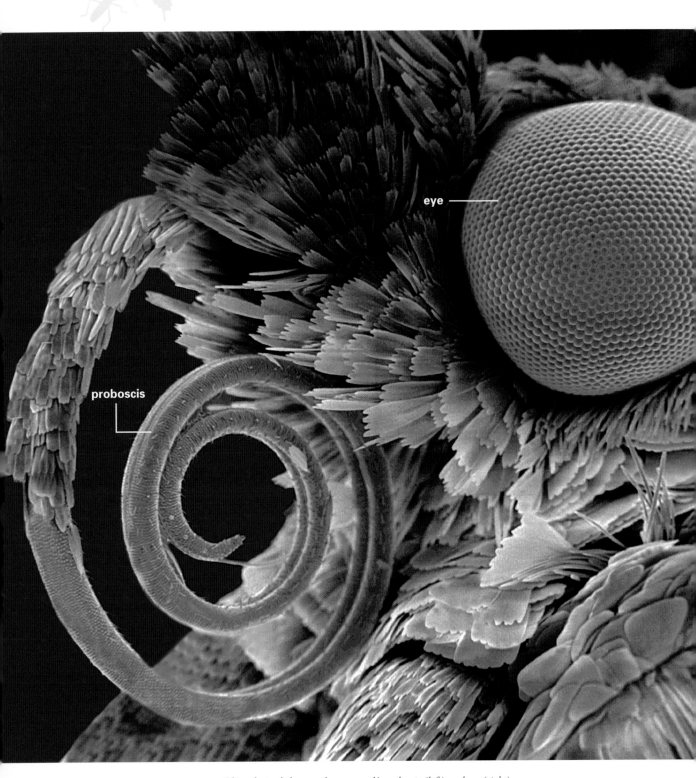

eye

proboscis

This colorized close-up shows a moth's proboscis (left) and eye (right).

range of light from violet to red, or the colors of a rainbow. Ultraviolet light is beyond the range of human eyesight. A moth's eyes allow it to see predators, find food, and, most importantly, find a mate. The antennae are sense organs used for touch and smell.

The proboscis is a long tube used like a tongue. It is hollow and allows the moth to suck up liquids. Most moths suck nectar from flowers, but some are known to suck urine and water from puddles. Adult tussock moths do not feed at all, but a species of Calpe moth from Asia sucks blood like a vampire!

The thorax is the middle section of the moth. Three pairs of legs attach to the thorax, and the tips serve as taste organs. Because the wings spread out from the thorax, a moth's strongest muscles are found in that area of the body. A network of veins lies between the two layers of **membrane** that make up the wings.

The abdomen contains most of a moth's bodily organs. This area holds the insect's **reproductive** organs, digestive organs, and organs to remove waste products. Moths, like many insects, do not have lungs. They breathe through tiny holes, called **spiracles**, on either side of the thorax and abdomen.

REPRODUCTION

The life cycle of a moth is an excellent example of complete **metamorphosis**. The life cycle begins as an egg, develops into a **larva**, pupates, then emerges as an adult moth.

Adult moths have one goal in life: mating. They emerge from their cocoons and immediately seek out mates. The females give off a chemical scent called a **pheromone** that tells the males, "Here I am." The scent of the European emperor female can be detected up to 11 kilometers (7 miles) away, and males fly fast to the source of that scent.

The female must lay her eggs quickly. Adult moths have short life spans, and the female wants to ensure that her species is carried on through her young. Some females use their **ovipositors** to carefully deposit each egg in a specific location. Other females broadcast, or spread their eggs like sowing grass seed in a field. The number of eggs depends on the species and how safe the eggs are once laid. The hepialid moth lays up to 18,000 eggs, each smaller than the head of a pin. Some females lay as few as 20 eggs.

Some females glue their eggs to the underside of leaves, thereby hiding them. Others cover their eggs with colored coatings, and the brown-tail moth covers her eggs with stinging hairs. Ghost moths lay their eggs in roots

or tree trunks, while yucca moths lay eggs in the ovaries of the yucca flower. The moth pollinates the flower. The flower's seeds feed the moth's larvae.

A yucca moth puts its eggs inside the yucca flower.

A six-spot burnet moth caterpillar stays in its cocoon during the pupa stage.

Moth eggs are laid on their favorite food source. Within a week, the egg darkens, and a tiny larva appears. It immediately eats its first meal—its own eggshell. From then on, the larva undertakes a single-minded pursuit to eat as much as it can as quickly as it can. As the caterpillar grows, it sheds its skin and enters the next stage of larva development. Each stage is called an instar. A caterpillar will go though several instars as it develops.

At some point, usually after about a month, the caterpillar larva has reached the appropriate size to enter the pupa stage. The caterpillar finds a suitable branch, twig, or underside of a leaf. It spins a silken pad that attaches to its tail. Slowly, it winds a loop or girdle to act as a support. Then, a cocoon is spun to enclose the caterpillar. This new stage, called the pupa stage, is the time when the caterpillar's body changes completely and becomes an adult moth. When the caterpillar is in the pupa, it is said to be pupating.

When the pupa stage is underway, the caterpillar's body parts are basically rearranged to become a moth. The pupa stage may last only a few days or many months. The length of time depends on the species. Shortly before the moth emerges,

Who Said That?

"There was a moth in there, and it still had its wings crumpled up, and it was just starting to pump its wings up. Life continues in lots of places, and life is a magical thing."
—Laurel Clark, American astronaut, on seeing a moth emerge from its cocoon

An emperor moth emerges from its cocoon.

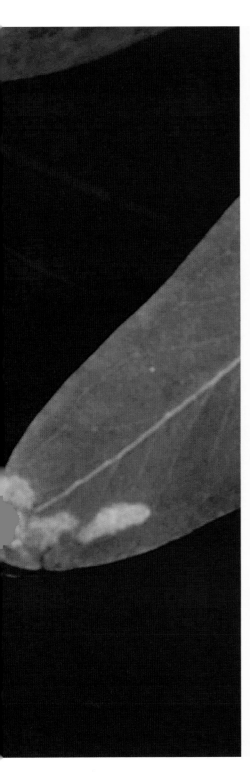

the pupa case becomes clear. The moth is visible through the case.

It is time for a new adult moth to emerge. It eats its way out of its case. It rests, often upside-down, pumping blood into its wings and waiting for the wings to harden. Unless the moth is patient, it will end up with crumpled, deformed wings. Once the wings are firm, the moth flutters and takes off. It is time to look for a mate. The cycle of life begins again.

During each stage of its development—egg, larva, pupa, and adult—moths are prime menu items for a number of predators. Night fliers worry about bats, while day fliers worry about birds. Dozens of species, particularly spiders, flies, wasps, and beetles, feed on eggs, caterpillars, or pupae. There are thousands of moth species, and critters to eat every species at every stage of development.

Chapter Three

Moths, Moths, and More Moths

Moths belong to the order *Lepidoptera,* a huge insect order with nearly 200,000 species. About 180,000 species are moths, while the rest are butterflies. The name *Lepidoptera* is Greek for "scaly wings," and that is the reason that moths feel "dusty." The dust rubbed off a moth's wing as a finger passes over it is really scales.

Scientists know that moths have been around for at least 100 million years. Captured in pieces of amber from Lebanon, parts of moth bodies have survived all that time. Moths and butterflies are so fragile that their bodies fall apart easily, so fossil records of whole moths are rare. Science can only prove 100 million years of moth existence. Perhaps new discoveries of older fossils will show that moths have survived longer.

Moths live in all types of habitats. Buckthorn hawk-moths hover to drink nectar from cactus blossoms in the

desert. Brilliant coppery dysphanias prefer the lush blooms of tropical jungles. Large oak eggars can be found in forests, while io moths flutter among farm crops. Among the thousands of moth species, most are night fliers, but some, such as eight-spotted foresters, spotted tigers,

The Madagascan sunset moth lives in tropical forests.

A puss moth caterpillar tries to scare away predators.

and large agaristas, fly in daylight. Their brilliant coloring makes them look more like butterflies than moths.

With many natural predators, moth species have developed defenses at all stages of life. Eggs are often glued to the underside of leaves or are leaf-colored so they can hide in plain sight. Caterpillars—moth larvae—must defend themselves from dozens of predators. Some have hideous sharp spines that keep predators away. Others eat poisonous leaves and become poisonous themselves. Distasteful caterpillars usually have colorful markings that shout "don't eat me!" Other caterpillars get protection from ants. The ants fend off predators, and, in return, the caterpillars discharge honeydew, sweet feces that ants find delicious. Some caterpillars, like the puss moth caterpillar and the lobster moth caterpillar, take on threatening postures and frighten away their enemies.

Coloration among adults often works as **camouflage**. Carpenter moths and tulip tree beauties **mimic** the colors of tree bark, while other moths, such as Millais tiger moths, mimic the colors of poisonous butterflies. The spotted sphinx, fiery campylotes, and the Madagascan sunset moth bear colors that warn birds and other predators that this prey is distasteful.

Mexican Jumping Beans

For years, novelty and joke shops sold Mexican jumping beans. These oddities are not always from Mexico, do not jump, and are not beans. They are sections of seeds, called carpels, in which a moth larva grows, pupates, and, eventually, emerges as a small gray moth.

The moth, *Laspeyresia saltitans,* lives only a short time. During the spring and summer, females find males and mate. They lay their eggs on green, undeveloped ovaries of the female flowers of a desert shrub. The eggs hatch and the tiny larvae bore into the capsules that hold the plant's future seeds.

As the seeds grow, the larvae feed on the pulp inside. The larvae thrive within the seed compartment. When the seeds are fully mature, they drop to the ground and split into thirds. Each third is called a carpel, and some of those carpels house moth larvae. These so-called beans wiggle and shake because the larvae heave themselves against the sides of the carpel shell. This action may happen to get the seed case out of direct sun. However, the seeds bounce about even in shadows.

Before a larva pupates, it cuts a small circular hatch inside the shell. Once the pupa stage ends, the moth knocks through the hatch and emerges. Then the life cycle of the Mexican jumping bean begins again.

Coloration can provide another form of defense. Owl moths, io moths, and cecropia moths have "eyespots." Eyespots fool predators into thinking they are facing larger, fiercer species, like an owl.

MAJOR MOTH SUPERFAMILIES

Considering there are up to 180,000 moth species, sorting these winged wonders into groups requires knowing how specific species are similar. Forty-four superfamilies divide moths into manageable numbers. Some families are quite large, with thousands of related species.

The spots on an io moth's wings can help scare away predators.

The largest moth family is the Noctuidae (nahk-TOO-ih-dee) with 25,000 species. These are hardy, drab-colored night fliers, and yet some noctuid moths are startlingly beautiful. The giant agrippa is a large moth with detailed patterns in browns and whites. Its relative, the black witch, is dark brown with complex patterns from dark to light shading from the outer wings toward the body.

Another large superfamily is the Geometridae (gee-OH-meh-trih-dee) with between 15,000 and 20,000 species. Geometrid caterpillars are inchworms. When they move, they "inch" along as if they are measuring leaves and twigs. The peppered moth's larva feeds at night, but during the day it poses as a motionless brown twig.

Fluttering colors mark the arctiid (ark-TEE-ihd) moths as highly distasteful. Many of the family's caterpillars feed on poisonous plants, storing the poison in their systems. The poison stays in the body, making the adult moth unpleasant for snacks. Arctiid moths often feature orange-and-black tiger markings, and many bear the word "tiger" in their common names. Two arctiid beauties that are not tiger moths are the giant leopard moth and the stunning crimson speckled moth.

Among the most attractive moth species are members of the Saturniidae (sah-tur-NEYE-ih-dee). These are

extra large species with brilliant colors, such as the vivid
yellow golden emperor and the orange-yellow male io
moths. Some saturniid moths have swallowtails, similar
to those on butterflies. The tails flutter behind the moth
and attract predators that often go away with a bite of
tail, leaving the moth to fly another day. The Indian moon
moth and the African moon moth have these deceptive
tails and are among the most attractive moths.

The giant leopard moth is a part of the arctiid family.

Moths come in a variety of colors, sizes, and styles. More primitive species—those that evolved earlier in time—tend to be smaller in size. Larger species are generally more recent on the biological evolution ladder. Collectors admire moths and put them on display. In many places throughout the world, however, moths and their caterpillars mean food, money, or both.

The giant atlas moth is one of the bigger moth species.

Chapter Four

In Appreciation of Moths

The Bisa people of Zambia depend on *chipumi* and *mumpa* for food and cash. *Chipumi* is the caterpillar of the speckled emperor moth *(Gynanisa maja)*. *Mumpa* is *gonimbrasia zambesina* moth larvae. These two moth species have such great value to the Bisa people that their harvesting became a ritual.

The head chief of the region ensures that the Bisa follow strict harvesting rules. In September, the moths begin to lay eggs, and scouts locate the areas where eggs are most plentiful. In a community ceremony, the chief covers a tribal shrine with a white cloth, then tears the cloth in half. Half the cloth remains with the shrine, while the other half is torn into thin strips. The chief's grandsons tie the strips to the trees with the most eggs, and the village waits. Shortly after the larvae hatch, a small sample is offered at the shrine.

When the caterpillars are at their plumpest, Bisa women and children harvest them. Only caterpillars from marked trees can be taken. The chief sets the price for the caterpillars, roughly $5 US per gallon. The village shares in the wealth the caterpillar harvest brings.

Many cultures around the world savor the flavor of moth larvae. In southern Africa, the red, yellow, and black markings of the Mopane larva make this caterpillar an attractive meal. They are

Would You Believe?
Caterpillars often provide more protein and better nutrition than equal amounts of beef or fish. Humans can get more energy from eating caterpillars than from eating soybeans, corn, or beef. Caterpillars are a good food source!

The mopane caterpillar is a popular snack in southern Africa.

sold dried and, according to those who eat them, taste like nuts. In northeastern India, delicious silkworm caterpillars are sold at a higher price than the silk their cocoons produce.

In national forests in many African nations, governments allow native people to harvest caterpillars for food and profit. These people need the protein provided by a caterpillar dinner. Leftover caterpillars are fried and sold at roadside stands to travelers looking for a snack.

Aborigines in Australia have eaten wittchety grubs for hundreds of years.

FOLKTALES AND SUPERSTITIONS

It is easy to imagine ancient moths flitting around the campfires of cave dwellers. After all, they swoop around backyard lights, street lamps, and candle flames today. What draws moths to the light? No one actually knows, although some scientists believe moths confuse the light for moonlight. Whatever the reason, moths are fascinated by light, and humans are fascinated by moths.

The hawkmoth *Acherontia atropos* spurred the imaginations of Europeans long ago. They saw markings on the moth's back that look like a skull and nicknamed this creature the death's-head moth. Death's-head moths make horrid creaking noises, which only added to its reputation for being connected to evil spirits.

Have you every heard of woolly bears and their role in predicting winter weather? Woolly bears are actually moth caterpillars, representing about 2,000 moth species. Nature watchers know that when the woolly bear caterpillars settle down for a long sleep, winter weather is on the way.

Another type of moth caterpillar, *Isia isabella,* is also thought to be a weather predictor. This caterpillar is black at either end with a red band on its middle. Some people believe that the narrower

Did You Know?
The island nation of Fiji honored hawkmoths with a six-stamp issue featuring hawkmoths from the islands. Thick-bodied, powerful fliers, hawkmoths inspired an airplane manufacturer to name a biplane the Tiger Moth.

the red band on the caterpillars, the longer and colder the winter will be. A wide band predicts mild winter weather.

Folktales, fables, and forecasting aside, the relationship between moths and humans has not always been a happy one. Moths may be beautiful and delicate. They can also be destructive.

Some people find the death's-head moth scary because of its strange markings and its unusual sounds.

Chapter Five

Man and Moths

In the late 1800s, some clever Americans decided to bring gypsy moths to the United States. They planned to breed the gypsies with silk moths, thus starting a silk industry in America. Unfortunately, the experiment was a disaster. The planned silk industry flopped, and the gypsy moths thrived. American forests had no natural predators for gypsy moths, and the moths began destroying forests. It is never a good idea to upset the balance of nature.

Scientists have tried introducing a solution to the gypsy moth problem—the calosoma beetle. Calosomas prey on gypsy moth larvae. The hope is that these insects and others that normally attack gypsy moth larva, such as flies, wasps, and beetles, will help control the gypsy moth population, along with birds and mammals that prey on the moths. It is also hoped that calosoma beetles do not become a problem on their own.

POLLINATORS AND PESTS

Moths fulfill a purpose in the natural

Did You Know?
In Victorian times, homemakers read Mrs. Beeton's *The Book of Household Management.* Mrs. Beeton recommended camphor, tobacco leaves, or bog-myrtle to ward off the munching of clothes moth caterpillars. Camphor is a strong-smelling mixture used in moth balls. Bog-myrtle is an herb that does the same thing.

Gypsy moths lay their eggs inside a tree.

world. As part of the cycle of life, they feed on plants and provide food for dozens of species. While drinking nectar, moths collect pollen from flowers. They help pollinate many nut-, seed-, and fruit-bearing plants.

Unfortunately, most people consider moths to be pests. Moth larvae destroy crops and can kill trees by eating all the leaves, burrowing in tree bark, and munching fruit and seeds. That worm found on an ear of corn—it's a moth caterpillar. Cabbage moth caterpillars devour cabbage leaves. The American copperwing caterpillar is a particular pest in apple orchards. Ipsilon dart caterpillars have a wider menu—munching their way through potato, tobacco, cabbage, and cotton plants. Moths also eat clothes, chewing their way through wool, cotton, and linen.

Despite their obvious negatives, moths fulfill their roles in nature's cycle of life. Flies, wasps, birds, lizards, and beetles feed on moths. That is the way of nature. Moths pollinate flowers, and lay their eggs. Other creatures feed on the eggs, larvae, or moths. Those creatures are food for still larger predators, and even the largest die. Their corpses feed other animals and enrich the soil, feeding the plants that will nourish the same larvae that become moths. The cycle is complete.

Moths help pollinate plants and serve as a food source for other animals.

Glossary

abdomen (AB-doh-men) the lower section of an insect body

antennae (an-TEN-nee) thin, sensory organs found on the heads of many insects

camouflage (KAM-oo-flaj) the devices that animals use to blend in with their environment

facet (FAA-set) any of the separate lenses that make up an insect's eye

larva (LAHR-vuh) worm-like stage of the life cycle of insects that develops into the pupa stage; the plural is *larvae* (LARH-vee)

membrane (MEM-brayn) a layer of living tissue

metamorphosis (meht-uh-MOR-foh-sis) a complete change in body form as an animal changes into an adult

mimic (MIH-mik) to copy the look or actions of another

ommatidia (ahm-muh-TIHD-ee-uh) the visual facets, or lenses, of an insect eye

ovipositors (oh-vih-PAHZ-ih-turz) tubular organs at the end of the abdomen of female insects and other species, used for laying eggs

pheromone (FAIR-uh-mohn) chemical substance made by an animal to attract mates or to create trails for others of the species to follow

proboscis (pro-BAHS-is) the long, flexible, tubular mouthpart of some insects

pupa (PYOO-puh) the insect stage during which an immature larva develops into an adult; the plural is *pupae* (PYOO-pee)

reproductive (ree-pro-DUK-tiv) having to do with producing young

spiracle (SPEER-uh-kul) a small opening in the side of an insect, used for breathing

thorax (THOR-aks) the middle body section of an insect, crustacean, or spider

For More Information

Watch It

Bug City: Butterflies & Moths. DVD, VHS. (Wynnewood, Penn.: Schlessinger Media, 1998.)

Insectia, Vol. 1 and 2. VHS. (Montreal: Imavision Distribution, 2002.)

Life in the Undergrowth. DVD. (Burbank, Calif.: BBC Video, 2006.)

Read It

Carter, David. *Smithsonian Handbooks: Butterflies and Moths.* New York: Dorling Kindersley Publishing, 2002.

McEvey, Shane F. *Moths and Butterflies.* Broomall, PA: Chelsea House Publications, 2001.

Preston-Mafham, Ken. *The Secret World of Butterflies and Moths.* Chicago: Raintree Publishing, 2002.

Whalley, Paul. *Eyewitness: Butterfly & Moth.* New York: Dorling Kindersley Publishing, 2000.

Winner, Cherie. *Everything Bug.* Minnetonka, MN: NorthWord Books for Young Readers, 2004.

Look It Up

Visit our Web site for lots of links about moths:
http://www.childsworld.com/links

Note to Parents, Teachers, and Librarians: We routinely verify our Web links to make sure they are safe, active sites—so encourage your readers to check them out!

The Animal Kingdom
Where Do Moths Fit In?

Kingdom: Animalia
Phylum: Arthropoda
Class: Insecta
Order: Lepidoptera

Genus and Species: 180,000 or more species
Relatives: caddisflies

Index

About the Author

Sophie Lockwood is a former teacher and a longtime writer. She writes textbooks, newspaper articles, and magazine articles. Sophie enjoys writing about animals and their habits. The most interesting part of her research, Sophie says, is learning how scientists apply their knowledge to save endangered species. She lives with her husband in the foothills of the Blue Ridge Mountains.